WALK

 :15 BEG
 :30 INT
 :45 ADV

©primalplay.com 2018

ANIMAL MOVES

JUNIOR FITNESS DECK

WWW.PRIMALPLAY.COM

TABLE OF CONTENTS

INTRODUCTION

ANIMAL MOVES
JUNIOR FITNESS DECK
PLAYING GUIDE

Copyright / Disclaimer

Copyright Text: © 2019 Darryl Edwards.
ISBN: 978-0-9933298-7-6
Explorer Publishing

PRIMALPLAY.COM

ANIMAL MOVES JUNIOR FITNESS DECK PLAYING GUIDE

Games created because exercise can be boring!

This booklet is a companion guide designed to give parents, teachers, daycare providers and youth coaches additional ideas to make the most of the ***Animal Moves Junior Fitness Deck**** and to get your kids to have more fun with fitness!

- **More Fun:** these additional ideas give you more innovative, practical and fun ways to move with the junior fitness deck.
- **It Works Right Away:** limited equipment and resources are needed to get going, reducing the barriers to movement.
- **Over 70 Game Ideas**: innovative challenges, games and activities to increase the frequency that the deck can be used throughout the day.

* Animal Moves Junior Fitness Deck – the simple card game that utilises the primal movements of the animal kingdom as inspiration to move for boys and girls.

ANIMALMOVESDECK.COM

WHY
MOVE LIKE
AN ANIMAL?

WHY ANIMAL MOVES?
MAKE THEM PART OF YOUR PLAY EXPERIENCE

Animal Moves are as old as movement is for humans. After all, we are animals right?

As adults, *Animal Moves* help to strengthen, condition and mobilise. They can make you more functional, more capable and encourage you to embrace your inner child as an adult. At its essence it is playful movement that we get the opportunity to indulge in as adults.

For children, it will help to *maintain* intrinsic motivation by playing games with movement. Most kids find *Animal Moves* more engaging than conventional forms of *'exercising'*, mainly because they can ultimately focus on having fun with physical challenges rather than just fitness training.

HOW MUCH ACTIVITY SHOULD OUR KIDS DO?
IT MAINLY DEPENDS ON THE AGE OF THE CHILD

BABIES

Babies should be encouraged to be physically active throughout the day except when sleeping.

TODDLERS/YOUNG CHILDREN (UNDER 5)

Children should be physically active for at least three hours a day and should not be inactive for lengthy periods except when they are sleeping.

CHILDREN/TEENS (5-17)

At least 60 minutes of physical activity daily which ranges from moderate to vigorous activity. Three days a week should cover vigorous aerobic activity.

Three days a week should incorporate resistance activities that build strong muscles and bones, such as playing tag or jumping like a kangaroo.

5 BENEFITS OF ANIMAL MOVES

#1 - Animal Moves Are Fun And FUNctional

These moves are inspired by the animal kingdom, however it isn't just about having fun, they encourage kids to engage in movement patterns often neglected in the modern environment. Kids need to be encouraged to move instead of spending their time predominately sitting.

Gross motor skills are such an important part of the healthy development for children. Gross motor activities not only get them active and allow them to release much needed nervous energy, it helps children regulate their sensory needs too.

The feature of animal movements to include crawls, jumps, sprawls and hops mean they move as nature intended, primally, naturally and functionally.

#2 - Animal Moves Can Make Adults Play More

It may have been quite a while (since childhood) that you last moved and played mimicking other animals. Once you get over any initial anxiety about being a grownup doing *Bunny Hops*, then you'll quickly see that these animal moves – all modelled on the movements of animals in the wild – can make a big difference to your health.

They are also a playful and pleasurable way to spend time with your kids too. You can participate in their pursuits and play with them - rather than just spectating.

There is an adult version of the Animal Moves Deck available too so you can make it even more of a family affair and combine both decks for more of a challenge.

#3 - Animal Moves Can Build Strength

What many of these animal movements have in common is that they require kids to support their full body weight, which is why they can be useful for building strong muscles, bones and joints.

The *Crab Walk* exercise, for example, aids in core stability and also builds strength throughout the shoulders, abs, hips and back. For added explosive power in the legs they can try out the *Frog Jump* card. There are plenty of options available for the kids to explore what their bodies are capable of in fun but challenging ways.

#4 - Animal Moves Are Great For The Brain

As you might have guessed, some of these movements such as the *Bear Crawl* require quite a bit of coordination to pull off. Even simpler animal movements like the *Flamingo Pose* help with overall coordination, balance and stability. These movements stimulate lots of brain activity.

Crawling - a quadrupedal movement where you rely on all four limbs for cross-body movement has significant benefits for the brain because left-right brain coordination challenges the brain and enhances learning. These crawling motions are good for the brain as well as the body.

#5 - Animal Moves Can Be Done Anyplace, Anywhere

You don't need access to a gym or any special equipment. You just need a location with enough room to move, indoors or outdoors. Your kids will realise their body is the best piece of equipment they own and the world around them is an ideal playground.
.

THE GAMES

SIMPLE
(ONE OR MORE KIDS)

Select a number of **Animal Moves Junior Deck** cards to play. Perform each card with 10-20 seconds rest between each move.

SHORT EIGHT BY 8
(ONE OR MORE KIDS)

Select 8 **Animal Moves Junior Deck** cards and perform eight repetitions for each move. For more of a challenge do not rest between cards.

DOUBLE TROUBLE
(ONE OR MORE KIDS)

Double the number of reps (or double the time) stated on the **Animal Moves Junior Deck** cards for the entire session.

STRIKE A POSE
(ONE OR MORE KIDS)

Select all **Animal Moves Junior Deck** POSE cards and get the kids to focus on being as still as possible and to breathe deeply throughout.

MOVEMENT SNACK
(ONE OR MORE KIDS)

Pick an **Animal Moves Junior Deck** card on the hour every hour during the day and perform the selected move. This will help to develop a habit of movement for the entire day.

HEADS OR TAILS
(FOR TWO KIDS)

Each child flips *Animal Moves Junior Deck* cards in the air simultaneously. The child whose card lands face up performs the movement on the card. The child whose card lands face down gets to rest.

If both cards are face up then perform both activities one after the other.

If both cards fall face down then both children rest for 15 seconds.

If both cards fall face down twice in succession then turn the cards over and perform both activities one after the other.

ANIMALYMPICS
(TWO OR MORE KIDS)

Set up a finish line 20 metres/yards away (or a distance of your choice) from the home base. Let the kids choose a card from the *Animal Moves Junior Deck* of animals that can crawl or walk (such as the *Crab Walk*, *Bear Crawl, Rabbit Walk, Alligator Walk*, etc.) and race against each other to the 20 metre/yards mark.

You can also try racing with other movement patterns such as jumping - for example, *Kangaroo Jump, Frog Jump* and *Flea Jump* for the same distance.

To mix things up you could try racing different animals and take the opportunity to discuss with the kids why certain animal moves are easier to cover a given distance than others.

OBSTACLE COURSE
(ONE OR MORE KIDS)

Set up an obstacle course indoors or outdoors. Set up sections that require children to climb over, run around, run over, climb under or jump over obstacles. At each obstacle perform the **Animal Moves Junior Deck** card assigned to it.

Be imaginative, be creative.

Get the kids involved in creating the play environment – cushions, chairs, broomsticks indoors or whatever the natural playground offers.

RELAY
(TWO OR MORE KIDS)

Set up a marker 20 metres/yards (or a distance of your choice) away from the home base. Run to the marker, select a card from the **Animal Moves Junior Deck**, perform the exercise and run back to the home base. Tag the next child until all children have completed the task.

JOIN IN WITH THE KIDS
(FAMILY OR GROUP ACTIVITY)

Perform the selected activity jointly as a parent, teacher or coach with the kids. Pay attention to the movement patterns that are easier for children to do, as opposed to the adults.

Discuss with the kids why that is likely to be the case. What can be done to improve the adult's ability? What can be done to develop the child's ability?

FLOATERS
(TWO OR MORE KIDS)

Drop several *Animal Moves Junior Deck* cards from eye level and skip any of the cards that land face up, perform moves for the face down cards.

BACKWARDS DRILL
(ONE OR MORE KIDS)

Select a number of locomotion cards including crawls, jumps and hops. Perform the movement on the cards but move backwards instead of going forwards.

SIDEWAYS DRILL
(ONE OR MORE KIDS)

Select several locomotion cards including crawls, jumps and hops. Perform the movement as described but traverse sideways instead of moving forwards. This will present quite a coordination challenge for some of the moves.

ADD SOUND
(ONE OR MORE KIDS)

Add sound effects for the selected animal move, this could be the sound the animal makes or an environmental sound. Be imaginative.

GET DIRTY
(ONE OR MORE KIDS)

Perform *Animal Moves Junior Deck* moves outdoors in the dirt, in the mud, in the rain or in the snow. Get down and dirty!

45-CARD PICKUP
(GROUP ACTIVITY)

Divide into two groups. Throw an entire **Animal Moves Junior Deck** in the air and let the cards float everywhere and fall to the ground. One group collects the face down cards, the other group collects the cards facing up.

Once both groups have collected their cards then each group performs the moves on the cards; the group that finishes their cards first wins.

WILD CARD SANDWICH
(ONE OR MORE KIDS)

Sandwich in an **Animal Moves Junior Deck** card in between the 2 green wild cards and perform each card. With the wild cards choose a movement that compliments the sandwiched card.

COMMERCIAL BREAK
(ONE OR MORE KIDS)

While watching the TV during every commercial perform 2-3 **Animal Moves Junior Deck** cards during each break.

CREATE A STORY
(ONE OR MORE KIDS)

Pick an **Animal Moves Junior Deck** card. Perform the activity. Visualize the animal's environment as you move in a way that mimics the animal and its natural habitat as much as possible. Create a story around why the animal is moving the way it does.

EVERYONE COACHES
(GROUP ACTIVITY)

Place the group of children evenly spaced in rows and columns. Pass the *Animal Moves Junior Deck* from one child to the next. Each time a child receives the deck, they take out a card and lead the rest of the group in performing that movement.

Once they have led the activity the child passes the deck onto the next person.

HIDE AND SEEK
(GROUP ACTIVITY)

Place *Animal Moves Junior Deck* cards around the house. Children form two groups. Teams are sent to find cards and return back to the base. Perform the movement on the card and then return to find more cards. The group with the most cards wins.

LEAD THE FORMATION
(GROUP ACTIVITY)

Place a group of children evenly spaced in rows and columns. Choose a leader who selects an *Animal Moves Junior Deck* card at random and get the entire group to follow along.

BIG BEN
(ONE OR MORE KIDS)

Perform an *Animal Moves Junior Deck* card on the hour and for every fifteen minutes of the hour throughout the day.

COUNTDOWN
(GROUP ACTIVITY)

Set a timer for a given timeframe and see how many *Animal Moves Junior Deck* cards each group can complete before the timer runs out.

QUICK-QUICK
(ONE OR MORE KIDS)

Parent or coach selects cards in quick succession. Perform only 2 repetitions or 5 seconds of every *Animal Moves Junior Deck* card.

HOMEPLAY (NOT HOMEWORK)
(ONE OR MORE KIDS)

Each child takes home an *Animal Moves Junior Deck* card and performs the movement at home as part of their assignment. Over time children will have completed all the moves in the deck.

DOUBLE
(ONE OR MORE KIDS)

Select a number of *Animal Moves Junior Deck* cards for the kids to play. The kids perform each card, twice, with 15 seconds rest between each move.

TRIPLE
(ONE OR MORE KIDS)

Select a number of *Animal Moves Junior Deck* cards for the kids to play. The kids perform each card, three times, with 10 seconds rest between each move.

3, 5 or 7 QUESTIONS
(GROUP ACTIVITY)

Children try to guess *Animal Moves Junior Deck* cards by asking a maximum number of 3, 5 or 7, yes or no questions. The more questions needed to determine what the card is - the more repetitions to be completed for that card.

MATCH UP
(GROUP ACTIVITY)

This activity requires two *Animal Moves Junior Deck* packs to play this game. Split the group into two teams.

1. Leader of team #1 takes all the POSE cards from Deck #1 and places them face up in a row.
2. Team #2 (except the leader) performs the posture from the first POSE card in the row.
3. The leader of team #2 picks a card one at a time from the second deck and keeps picking cards until it matches the first pose card from Deck #1. At this point the remainder of the team rests for 15 seconds.
4. Continue the process until all the remaining POSE cards are matched.

Then Team #2 shuffles their Deck #2 cards and performs the role of Team #1 above.

MUSICAL MOVES
(GROUP ACTIVITY)

Play music and get the children to perform an *Animal Moves Junior Deck* card while it plays. When the music stops, everyone has to freeze and hold an animal pose. If you see someone moving, they're out. Last one playing wins!

TRAVEL ANIMAL MOVES
(GROUP ACTIVITY)

Create a contest that lists the most remote places that a child has used their *Animal Moves Junior Deck* card. Each group completes their list before the time runs out.

An additional task could have children take photos of themselves performing the moves in remote or obscure locations. Stay safe.

HOT POTATO
(GROUP ACTIVITY)

A pack of *Animal Moves Junior Deck* cards is passed around a group of 4 to 8 children sitting in a circle. When the coach or parent claps, whoever is holding the deck will select a card and perform the exercise.

Then continue passing the deck and continue the game for several rounds.

GUESS WHAT
(GROUP ACTIVITY)

Have everyone secretly write down the name of an animal from the *Animal Moves Junior Deck* on a small piece of paper or a "post-it" note. Then have them tape the name of the animal on the back of the person to their left.

Everyone goes around and asks people yes or no questions about what animal is on their back. They can only ask each person one question. The person who can do it in the least number of questions wins.

At the end of the game every person should perform the animal move of the person to their left for one minute. Rest as required.

ANIMALMOVESDECK.COM

COUNT OUT LOUD
(GROUP ACTIVITY)

Perform a move from the *Animal Moves Junior Deck*. For every rep you perform count out as loud as you can. This works very well in groups as it distracts everyone else causing the children to be more focused on what they are doing.

This confusion is great for the mind and the body.

COUNT BACKWARDS
(GROUP ACTIVITY)

Perform a move from the *Animal Moves Junior Deck*. For every rep you perform count backwards out loud. For example if doing 15 repetitions, count back from 15-to-1. If working in a group count out loud.

This is a great workout for the brain.

TIMES TABLES
(GROUP ACTIVITY)

Perform a move from the *Animal Moves Junior Deck.* For every rep you perform count in multiples of a certain number. For example, using the number 3 - if doing 15 repetitions count upwards out loud from 3-to-45 in multiples of three. If playing in a group count out even louder as a distraction to the other players.

This is another great workout for the brain!

PRIMALPLAY.COM

START EASY END TOUGH
(ONE OR MORE KIDS)

Starting on the first day of the month increase the number of *Animal Moves Junior Deck* cards performed by 1 card-a-day for one month. For example on day 1 you could start with 4 cards. Day 2 = 5 cards, Day 3 = 6 cards and so on until the end of the month. Day 31 = 35 cards.

WHEN AT HOME
(GROUP ACTIVITY)

Assign a movement to perform when certain events happen at home. For example, the child performs one *Animal Moves Junior Deck* card every time they watch a video online, or every time they go upstairs.

BECOME AN EXPERT
(ONE OR MORE KIDS)

Children should prepare a 5-minute oral presentation on one of the *Animal Moves Junior Deck* cards. Include a demonstration and detailed discussion on what makes up the movement pattern, and why it resembles the animal involved.

MOVEMENT SCIENTIST
(ONE OR MORE KIDS)

Get the children to work on a project that incorporates an educational objective. For example - students can talk about the muscles and joints used during an *Animal Moves Junior Deck* activity.

HEART SCIENTIST
(ONE OR MORE KIDS)

Children can work on a project that incorporates measurement and reporting. For example - students can measure the heart rate per minute before and after the movement performed on an *Animal Moves Junior Deck* card.

Students can note what movements increase the heart rate more than others and can even plot a graph to represent the numbers before and after using the deck.

OBSERVATION
(ONE OR MORE KIDS)

Children can work on a project that incorporates an educational objective. For example - students can report on physical activity that require similar movements as on the *Animal Moves Junior Deck* cards.

PARTNER UP
(TWO OR MORE KIDS)

Partner up and work on an *Animal Moves Junior Deck* card together in an interesting fashion in an interesting way. For instance, two children could perform the *Bunny Hop* back-to-back. Three children could hold hands while doing an *Air Squat*.

CHALLENGE THE PARENTS
(ONE OR MORE KIDS)

Pick a card. Engage in a competition against your parents.

CIRCLE DU SOLEIL
(GROUP ACTIVITY)

Children stand in a circle. An ***Animal Moves Junior Deck*** is passed from one child to the next. Each time the child gets the deck, they remove a card and lead the rest of the circle in performing the movement. Once completed pass the deck on to the person to your right and continue the process.

TREASURE HUNT
(ONE OR MORE KIDS)

Place ***Animal Moves Junior Deck*** cards around the home. Children are sent to find cards and return back to the base. Once all cards have been found perform the movements on those cards.

ANIMAL HUNT
(ONE OR MORE KIDS)

Place ***Animal Moves Junior Deck*** cards around the home. Children are sent to find cards but can only travel using certain Animal Moves such as a *Bear Crawl*. The game ends once all cards have been found.

TRANSITION
(ONE OR MORE KIDS)

Use the ***Animal Moves Junior Deck*** as a tool to transition or flow from one task to another. Perform a couple of cards in between routine activities to mix things up and make it fun.

GO WILDER
[TWO OR MORE KIDS]

Pick out the 2 Green *Animal Moves Junior Deck* wild cards. Create 2 animal moves that are not already covered by what else is in the deck. You can make this a group activity and award a prize for the team with the most imaginative animal and also an award for the top performance of that animal move.

ALIEN MOVE
[TWO OR MORE KIDS]

Pick out the 2 Green *Animal Moves Junior Deck* wild cards and get the kids to create 2 alien moves. You can make this a group activity and award a prize for the team with the most imaginative movement pattern created and a second award for the performance of the alien move that can be done most consistently by the children.

KITCHEN TABLE
[ONE OR MORE KIDS]

Place a few *Animal Moves Junior Deck* cards facedown on the kitchen table. When a parent calls for an animal moves break the child reveals their card and picks up one of the cards and performs the movement.

CREATE YOUR OWN
[ONE OR MORE KIDS]

Get the kids to create their own *Animal Moves Junior Deck* card. Draw the image, detail the movements and determine the time or the number of repetitions for beginner, intermediate and advanced.

PRIMALPLAY.COM

THROW THE DICE
(GROUP ACTIVITY)

The leader of team #1 rolls two dice. Select the number of cards from the *Animal Moves Junior Deck* that coincides with the number rolled. If the number rolled is an even one then both teams perform the moves on all the cards, if the number rolled is an odd number then only team #1 performs the moves.

Then leader of team #2 rolls the dice and continues with the game.

If a double number is rolled such as double 1 or double 2 the game ends.

KEEP SCORE
(TWO OR MORE KIDS)

Children receive points for every *Animal Moves Junior Deck* they complete over a week. Completion of each card equals one point. Keep a running total of each child's score.

BALANCE ON HEAD
(GROUP ACTIVITY)

Divide children into two relay teams. Set up a marker 20 metres/yards (or a distance of your choice) away from the home base. The kids walk as fast as they can to the marker and back to the base with a *Animal Moves Junior Deck* card balancing on their head.

If a card falls off a child's head while walking, the child must perform the movement before heading back. If the card drops twice or more then their team must perform the movement too.

The team that gets all of its members back first wins.

WALL CHALLENGE
(TWO OR MORE KIDS)

Children stand a few metres away from a wall and flick their *Animal Moves Junior Deck* card trying to get as close to the wall as possible. Whoever gets closest to the wall wins and the other person performs their card.

ANIMAL TRUMPS
(TWO OR MORE KIDS)

Children complete and accumulate a certain number of *Animal Moves Junior Deck* cards to earn group or individual awards. A range of cards are randomly made available at certain times. Children can trade cards by performing the moves of cards they would like to trade with other children who may have duplicate cards.

ANIMAL TRIVIA
(GROUP ACTIVITY)

Divide the children into groups of two teams. The coach asks a question related to one of the *Animal Moves Junior Deck* cards without naming the animal or describing the move itself. The team that answers the question correctly wins a point. Both teams perform the exercise.

ANIMAL MOVEATHON
(GROUP ACTIVITY)

Organise a fundraiser that raises money for charity based on the time spent doing *Animal Moves Junior Deck* cards as a group.

COOPERATION
[GROUP ACTIVITY]

Children receive a number of **Animal Moves Junior Deck** cards and must decide as a team which team member will perform what card and in what order. Cards must be equally divided between team members and each team member must complete their move before the next team member can begin.

ANIMAL MOVES LADDER
[GROUP ACTIVITY]

Perform 1 **Animal Moves Junior Deck** card on Monday, 2 on Tuesday, 3 on Wednesday and so on - end at 5 for Friday or 7 for Sunday.

ANIMAL MOVES REVERSE LADDER
[GROUP ACTIVITY]

Perform 7 **Animal Moves Junior Deck** card on Monday, 6 on Tuesday, 5 on Wednesday and end at 3 on Friday or 1 on Sunday.

ANIMAL CIRCUIT
[GROUP ACTIVITY]

Set up stations around the house, garden or park. Around 7 or so is a good number to begin with. Children rotate every 30 seconds from one **Animal Moves Junior Deck** card to the next with 30 seconds rest between each station.

OUT OF A HAT
[GROUP ACTIVITY]

Pick an **Animal Moves Junior Deck** at random out of a hat. A bonus prize for picking the *Rabbit Walk!*

FAVOURITE
[GROUP ACTIVITY]

Children pick and list their 3 favourite *Animal Moves Junior Deck cards* and deliver a 2-3 minute oral presentation as to why that is and what they could do to make those entries in the list even more fun!

FUNCTIONAL MOVES
[GROUP ACTIVITY]

Children select an *Animal Moves Junior Deck* card and discuss how this particular movement could help with day-to-day tasks.

BIRTHDAY GREETINGS
[GROUP ACTIVITY]

The Child who has a birthday selects an *Animal Moves Junior Deck* card and everyone does repetitions corresponding to their age. For example, a 10-year-old could celebrate 10 Bunny Hops and do them jointly with the group.

GO FOR A FUN RUN
[ONE OR MORE KIDS]

Go to your local park and run (or sprint) from tree to tree. At each tree perform an *Animal Moves Junior Deck* card, at each bench perform 2 cards, at a lamppost perform 3 cards. It's amazing how many cards you will cover even over short distances.

KEEP PLAYING

KEEP MOVING, KEEP PLAYING

1. It's unlikely you will play all the games in this guide, but there is no need to do so However, do try as many of them as possible so you can highlight your favourites. Hopefully, these ideas will spur you on to create more games of your own. Get the children involved; they indeed are a creative bunch when given the opportunity.

2. Playing these games and creating your variations will ensure you can extend the use of the *Animal Moves Junior Deck* beyond the simplest game of shuffle and go.

3. Get your kids invested in regular use of the deck and other physical activities too by focusing on movement as fun and games rather than as a chore.

4. Many of our children are not moving enough, whether at home or school so creating as many purposeful movement breaks or snacks as possible is one way to disrupt daily sedentary time. Five minutes here, two minutes there throughout the day soon adds up and can be a useful way to distract kids from the ever-increasing desire to stay connected virtually.

5. Don't think of these activities as purely physical. *Animal Moves* such as crawling or indeed any cross-body movement increases blood flow to the left and right side of the brain and boosts learning potential.

   In a recent survey, 88% of UK teachers said they believe that short bouts of coordination exercises can improve integration of left and right hemispheric brain function [Howard-Jones, P. A. (2014)]

HAVE FUN WITH MOVEMENT

PRIMALPLAY.COM

animalmovesdeck.com

Find out about other Animal Moves products including the Animal Moves adult deck at www.animalmovesdeck.com

animalmovesbook.com

Reconnect with the fitter, stronger and healthier you with the Animal Moves book. Use the primal movement program inspired by the animal kingdom to become king or queen of the jungle in no time!

ANIMAL MOVES – achieved Amazon #1 best-seller status in several categories

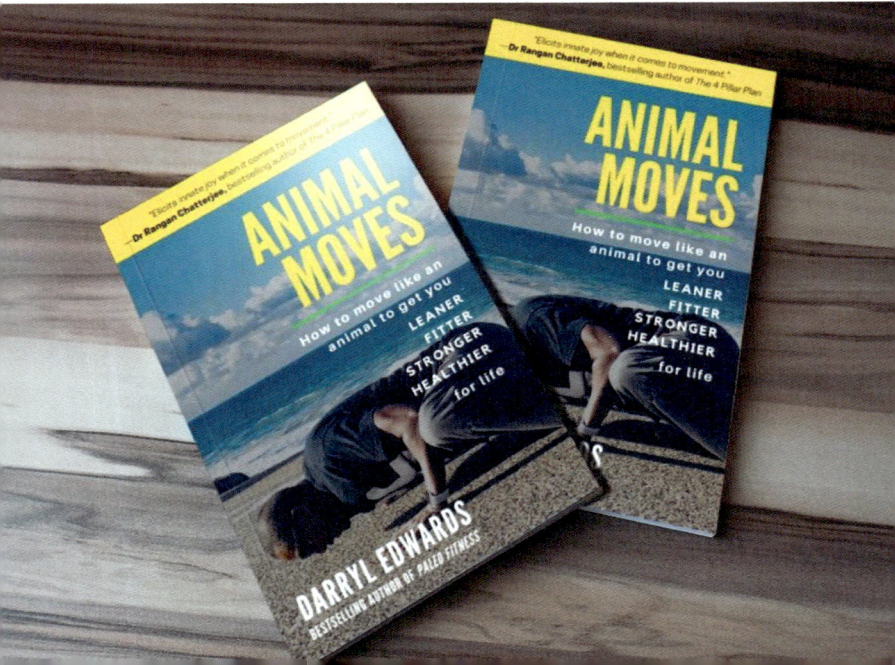

Printed in Poland
by Amazon Fulfillment
Poland Sp. z o.o., Wrocław